Extreme Sports

ROCK CLIMBING

Marie-Therese Miller, PhD

DiscoverRoo
An Imprint of Pop!
popbooksonline.com

abdobooks.com

Published by Pop!, a division of ABDO, PO Box 398166, Minneapolis, Minnesota 55439.

Printed in the United States of America, North Mankato, Minnesota.

052020
092020

THIS BOOK CONTAINS RECYCLED MATERIALS

Cover Photo: Shutterstock Images
Interior Photos: Shutterstock Images, 1, 7, 12, 18–19, 29, 30; iStockphoto, 5, 6, 8–9, 13 (top left), 13 (top right), 13 (middle left), 13 (middle right), 13 (bottom left), 13 (bottom right), 14, 15, 20, 22, 23, 27, 28, 31; ClassicStock/Alamy, 11; Tuomas Lehtinen/Alamy, 17; Ben Horton/National Geographic, 21; Ben Margot/AP Images, 25

Editor: Brienna Rossiter
Series Designer: Jake Slavik

Library of Congress Control Number: 2019954982

Publisher's Cataloging-in-Publication Data

Names: Miller, Marie-Therese, author.

Title: Rock Climbing / by Marie-Therese Miller, PhD

Description: Minneapolis, Minnesota : POP!, 2021 | Series: Extreme sports | Includes online resources and index.

Identifiers: ISBN 9781532167843 (lib. bdg.) | ISBN 9781532168949 (ebook)

Subjects: LCSH: Rock climbing--Juvenile literature. | Bouldering--Juvenile literature. | Extreme sports--Juvenile literature. | Sports--Juvenile literature.

Classification: DDC 796.046--dc23

WELCOME TO DiscoverRoo!

Pop open this book and you'll find QR codes loaded with information, so you can learn even more!

Scan this code* and others like it while you read, or visit the website below to make this book pop!

popbooksonline.com/rock-climbing

*Scanning QR codes requires a web-enabled smart device with a QR code reader app and a camera.

TABLE OF CONTENTS

CHAPTER 1
To the Top 4

CHAPTER 2
Rock Climbing History 10

CHAPTER 3
All Kinds of Climbing. 16

CHAPTER 4
Safety. 26

Making Connections. 30
Glossary 31
Index. 32
Online Resources 32

CHAPTER 1

TO THE TOP

A rock climber stands at the bottom of a cliff. She steps into her **harness** and buckles it. Then she ties a rope to it. She uses a double figure-eight knot. Next, she checks the knot. She makes sure it is tight and lies flat.

WATCH A VIDEO HERE!

Rock climbers learn to tie many kinds of knots. The double figure-eight knot is one of the most common.

Climbers look for small edges they can grip.

The climber checks to make sure her climbing partner is ready. Then she begins to climb. She carefully chooses where to place her hands and feet.

Down on the ground, her partner **belays**. He pulls the rope tight. That way, the rope will catch her if she falls.

DID YOU KNOW?

Before each climb, the climber asks, "On belay?" When ready, the partner replies, "Belay on."

A belay device acts like a brake. It catches the rope to stop the climber from falling.

Finally, the climber reaches the top of the cliff. She pauses to enjoy the view. Then it's time to come down. She sits

A rappel device allows climbers to slowly lower themselves down a rope.

back in her harness and straightens her legs. Her partner lowers her slowly as she walks down the rock.

CHAPTER 2

ROCK CLIMBING HISTORY

Rock climbing got its start in the late 1800s. W. P. Haskett Smith was one of the first rock climbers. In 1886, he climbed Napes Needle in England. Smith climbed without help from any equipment.

LEARN MORE HERE!

Two climbers scale the Alps in the mid-1900s.

However, many early climbers used ladders and pitons. A piton is a metal spike. A climber can hammer it into rock and use it to hold rope.

During World War II (1939–1945), soldiers climbed using aluminum **carabiners** and strong nylon ropes. After the war, people bought the leftover climbing equipment. The sport became safer and easier.

DID YOU KNOW?

Using equipment to climb is called aid climbing. In free climbing, people use equipment only for safety.

ROCK CLIMBING GEAR

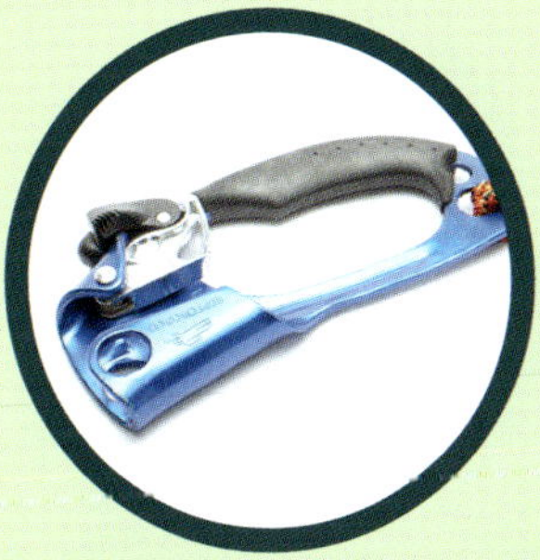

ascender: attaches to a rope so climbers can go up it

cam: removable anchor that slides into cracks

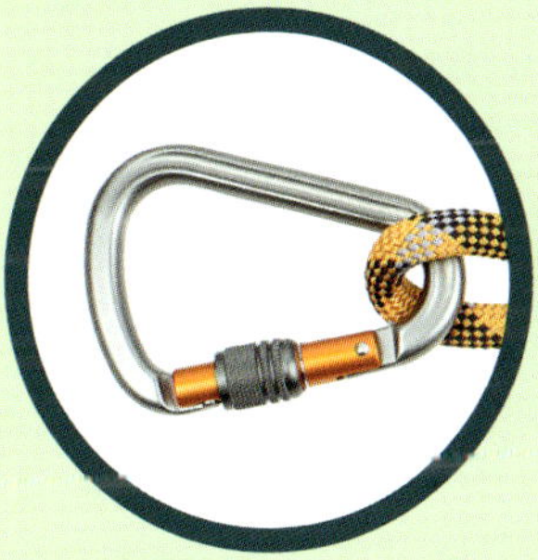

carabiner: clips ropes and equipment together

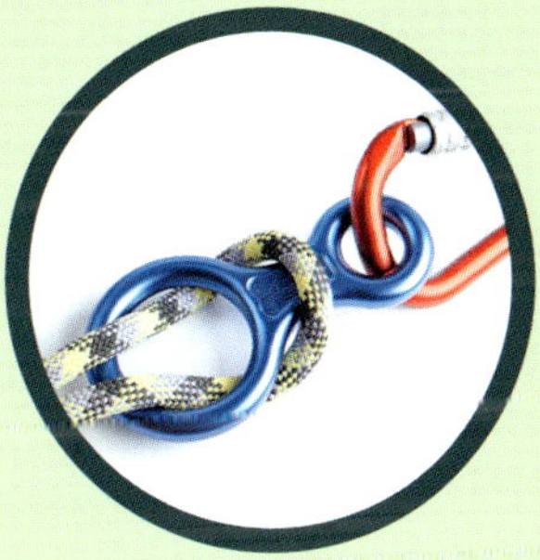

descender: helps lower climbers down a rope

nut: removable anchor that is wedged into rocks

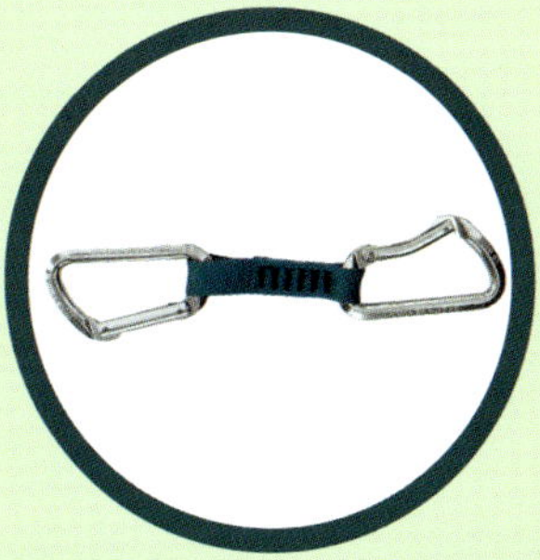

quickdraw: strap with two carabiners that clips ropes to protection devices

El Capitan is 3,000 feet (914 m) high.

YOSEMITE ROCK WALLS

Yosemite National Park in California has many huge rock formations. Two of the most famous are Half Dome and El Capitan. These rock walls are thousands of feet tall. And they are extremely steep. Climbers can use several routes to reach the top. Some routes take several days to complete. Climbers camp in tents on the side of the rock.

By the 1980s, climbing gyms began opening. These gyms have artificial

At gyms, climbers grip handholds attached to walls.

rock walls. Some climbers use them to practice for outdoor climbing. Others only climb indoors.

CHAPTER 3

ALL KINDS OF CLIMBING

Today, people enjoy many different types of climbing. Top-rope climbing has the rope anchored to the top of the climb. One end is tied to the climber's **harness**. The other end threads through a **belay** device on a partner's harness.

COMPLETE AN ACTIVITY HERE!

This cliff in Laos is a popular site for top-rope climbing.

Traditional climbers also use partners. The first climber places **protection devices** in the rock's cracks. This climber is called the leader. The leader also clips **carabiners** and rope to the devices. That way, the rope will keep both climbers from falling too far. The second climber removes the protection devices. The climbers will use them again on the next **pitch**.

In traditional climbing, partners place and remove protection devices as they climb.

In sport climbing, protection devices are permanently attached to the rock. Climbers clip their ropes to them as they climb.

Sport climbers use permanent anchors already placed along the climbing route.

When simul-climbing, the second climber is also moving. This increases the risk of falls.

DID YOU KNOW?

In several climbing styles, one partner belays while the other climbs. But in *simul-climbing*, both partners move at the same time.

Boulderers have spotters watch them. A spotter can move a falling climber toward the crash pad.

Boulderers do not use ropes or harnesses. Instead, they climb on low rocks. Crash pads go on the ground beneath the climbers. These foam mats help cushion any falls.

Free solo climbers don't use any ropes or safety devices. They often climb very high. A fall can be deadly.

The lack of protection devices makes free solo climbing incredibly risky.

SUPERSTAR

TOMMY CALDWELL

- Tommy Caldwell began rock climbing when he was three years old.
- In 1995, Caldwell won a sport climbing competition against adult expert climbers. He was just 16 years old.
- Caldwell saved his climbing group from kidnappers in Kyrgyzstan in 2000.
- Caldwell and his climbing partner, Kevin Jorgeson, were the first to free climb El Capitan's Dawn Wall route. It took them 19 days to reach the top.

Tommy Caldwell (right) and Kevin Jorgeson climb El Capitan in 2015.

- On June 6, 2018, Caldwell and another partner, Alex Honnold, set a new speed record for climbing the Nose route of El Capitan. They reached the top in 1 hour, 58 minutes, and 7 seconds.

CHAPTER 4

SAFETY

Rock climbing can be dangerous. But gear helps climbers stay safe. Helmets protect climbers' heads during falls. They also keep climbers safe from falling rocks or equipment. Climbers wear safety **harnesses** too.

LEARN MORE HERE!

For a proper fit, a harness must not slip down over the climber's hip bones.

DID YOU KNOW?

Many climbers use chalk. It dries their hands and keeps them from slipping.

Climbers can use their ropes to dangle from cliffs.

Climbers use ropes that can stretch a bit. These ropes help lessen the shock of falls. Climbers check their ropes and harnesses often for signs of wear.

Climbing shoes fit snugly. They help climbers feel the rock beneath their feet. And their sticky rubber soles grip the rock.

Many climbing shoes have a thin rubber layer over the heel and toes.

MAKING CONNECTIONS

TEXT-TO-SELF

Do you think you would make a good rock climber? Why or why not?

TEXT-TO-TEXT

Have you read other books about adventurous athletes? What do they have in common with the rock climbers described in this book?

TEXT-TO-WORLD

People enjoy climbing indoors and outdoors. How might climbing indoors be different from climbing outside?

GLOSSARY

belay – to secure a climber at the end of a rope.

carabiner – a metal ring with a spring hinge on one side that opens and closes. It can clip on to ropes, knots, and gear.

harness – safety equipment that fits around a climber's legs and waist. It is attached to rope to prevent falls.

pitch – one section of a climbing route.

protection device – any item that attaches to rock to serve as an anchor while climbing.

simul-climbing – a climbing technique where both partners are moving at the same time.

INDEX

belaying, 7, 16, 21

bouldering, 22

El Capitan, 14, 24–25

equipment, 10, 12–13, 26

free climbing, 12, 24

harness, 4, 9, 16, 22, 26, 28

shoes, 29

sport climbing, 20

top-rope climbing, 16

traditional climbing, 18

ONLINE RESOURCES
popbooksonline.com

Scan this code* and others like it while you read, or visit the website below to make this book pop!

popbooksonline.com/rock-climbing

*Scanning QR codes requires a web-enabled smart device with a QR code reader app and a camera.